XANDER NASH:

THE BEGINNING OF IT ALL

WRITTEN BY HUNTER TALEN
ILLUSTRATED BY NEIL KLEID

Published by Creation By Design, LLC, Teaneck, NJ
www.creationbydesign.com

Printed in: Canada
Cover & interior design: Creation By Design
Xander Nash and related characters by Creation By Design

ISBN: 978-0-9828077-4-3

Publisher's Cataloging-In-Publication Data
(Prepared by The Donohue Group, Inc.)

Talen, Hunter.
  Xander Nash. [1], the beginning of it all / written by Hunter Talen ; illustrated by Neil Kleid.

  p. : ill. ; cm.

  Includes index.
  ISBN: 978-0-9828077-4-3

  1. Bible stories, English--O.T.--Juvenile fiction. 2. Archaeology--Juvenile fiction. 3. Time travel--Juvenile fiction. 4. Bible stories--O.T.--Fiction. 5. Archaeology--Fiction. 6. Time travel--Fiction. 7. Adventure fiction. I. Kleid, Neil. II. Title. III. Title: Beginning of it all

PZ7.T3546 Xa 2010
[Fic]

Contents

The
Marshmallow That
Ate Cleveland

Chapter 1

Storm Clouds

"C'mon, Xander, we're gonna be late!"

Xander Nash looked at his watch.

"You're already late," he called to Kevin. "The movie started ten minutes ago."

Kevin peeked into his brother's bedroom. Xander was lying on his bed, reading a book.

"C'mon, Xander," Kevin pleaded. "We can still go. We'll just miss the beginning of the movie. It's no big deal. Nothing ever happens in the beginning anyway. All the really exciting stuff comes at the end."

Xander shot Kevin an annoyed look. "No, thank you," he said, returning to his reading.

Kevin persisted. "Tell you what," he said. "We'll watch the movie, and when it's over, we'll wait for the next showing to see the part we missed."

Xander shot his older brother another angry look. "No," he insisted. "That's too weird."

"*You're* weird," Kevin blurted. "All you ever do is read stupid books on history and exploring. If you're so interested in explorers, why don't you just quit school and become one?"

Xander made a face at his brother and said, "Because I'm only nine years old and in fourth grade, genius."

Kevin went downstairs and left the house, slamming the door behind him.

Xander shook his head. He was amused that Kevin had called him weird. After all, Kevin was the *king* of weird. When he ate pizza, Kevin would first scrape off all the cheese with a fork and swallow it in a big blob. Then he'd eat the crust separately. *That* was weird. Definitely weird!

Mom popped her head into Xander's bedroom and asked, "Alexander, what's all the commotion?"

Xander's parents were the only people who called him by his full name instead of his nickname.

Xander said, "It's nothing, Mom.

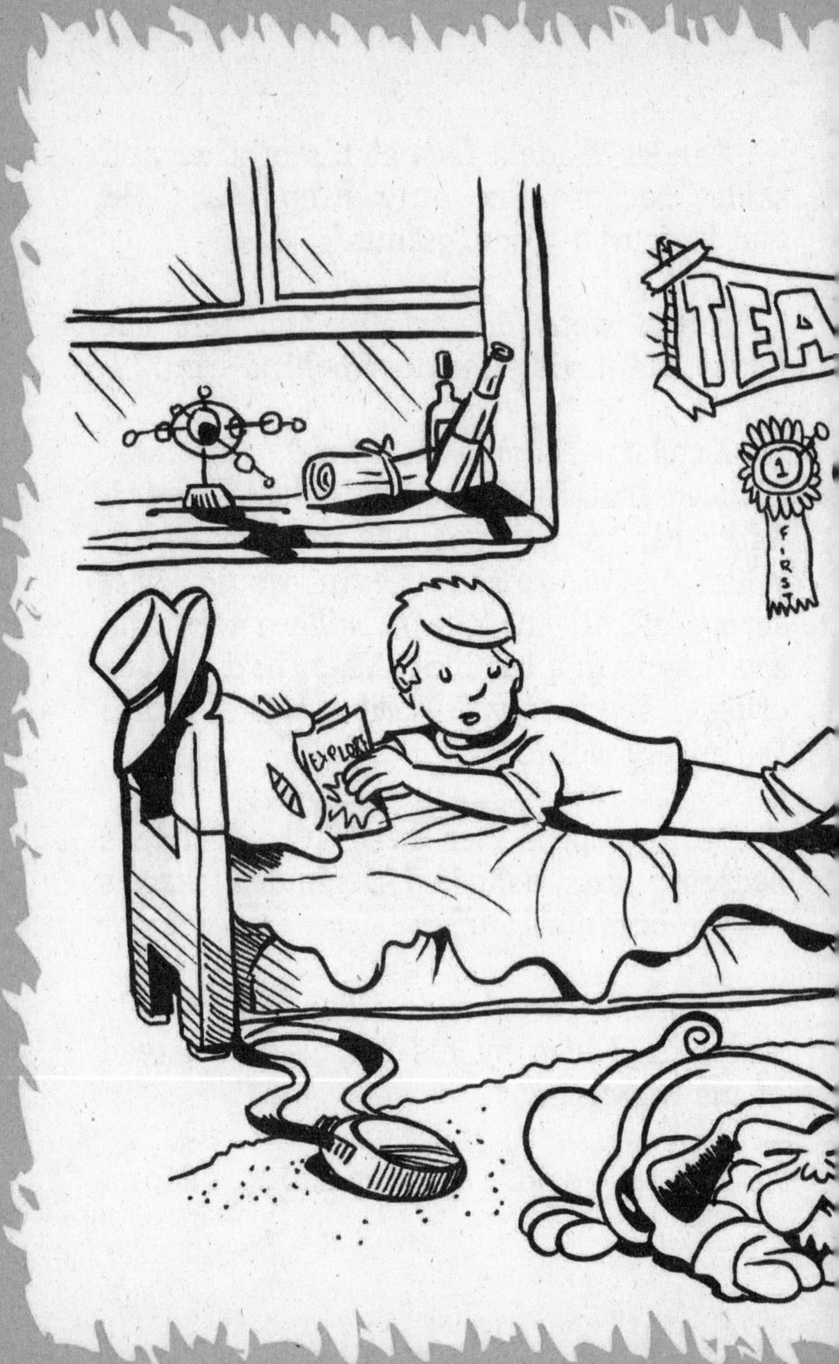
1
FIRST

Kevin just went to the Rialto, even though he's late, as usual."

Mom smiled. "Well, I hope he took his umbrella," she said. "It looks like it may rain soon. You should walk Mitts now, before the weather turns bad."

"Okay," Xander agreed.

He hated to stop reading, but he was always happy to do it for Mitts. Mitts was the best dog in the world. Xander had given him that name because each of the pug's four large paws reminded him of a baseball catcher's mitt.

Xander called for Mitts, who came running immediately.

"Good boy," Xander said, petting the dog's wrinkled face and curled tail. "At least *you* know how to be on time."

Xander put on his jacket and his favorite hat -- a brown fedora. He thought

6

it made him look like a real archaeologist.

Well, it DID make him look like a kid-sized version of his all-time movie hero, Michigan Jones. Ever since seeing *Riders of the Lost Arch* for the first time, he had known that he liked the look that Michigan Jones had about him.

But it wasn't just about the look. An archaeologist had to be equipped and ready for anything. So he also put on his explorer's belt. It held all of his trusty exploring equipment—a flashlight, a compass, a water canteen, and a folded map of the world. Xander was careful to carry these items whenever he went out. After all, he never knew where the exciting adventures of an archaeologist might lead him.

Xander also made sure he had his small writing pad, in case he needed to take notes on a sudden new discovery.

Finally, Xander fastened the leash on Mitts, who, eager to go walking, jumped up and down as the two started out the front door.

"Wait, Alexander," Mom said. "Take your umbrella, in case it starts to rain. And don't stay out too long."

"Okay, Mom," Xander said, grabbing his umbrella by the door.

He tugged gently on the leash. "C'mon, Mitts," he said.

The two walked outside along the sidewalk; Xander could see dark clouds gathering in the gloomy sky.

Mom's right, he thought. It *is* going to rain soon.

As they continued, Mitts tried to run ahead. He always did. But Xander held firmly to the leash.

"Not so fast, Mitts," Xander said. "Just do your business so we can get home."

At the corner, Mitts headed to a bush and lifted his leg.

Xander chuckled. Looks like the rain's already starting, he thought.

Xander and Mitts walked several more blocks. They passed the Rialto. A large sign showed the name of the movie playing there: *The Marshmallow That Ate Cleveland.*

"That sounds like Kevin's speed," Xander snickered.

Just then, a cluster of dark clouds formed overhead.

BOOM! A loud clap of thunder rocked the air.

Xander tugged at the dog's leash.

"C'mon, Mitts," he urged. "The rain is about to start. Let's get back home now."

As Xander turned around, he felt the first raindrops on his head. Quickly he opened his large umbrella.

The sudden storm had caught Xander by surprise. A heavy rain began to shower down on him. A strong wind blew against his face and body. Xander held tightly to his umbrella. It almost slipped out of his wet fingers, so Xander grabbed the handle with both hands.

That was a mistake.

Without thinking, Xander had let go of the leash. Mitts was suddenly free and began to run away.

Xander cried, "Mitts, come back! You're going the wrong way! We have to get back home *now*!"

Xander wasn't sure if Mitts could hear

him in the noisy downpour. Still clutching his umbrella, he chased after the dog while trying not to slip on the wet pavement.

After running several blocks, Xander finally caught up with Mitts. He bent down and grabbed the leash. Xander pulled the dog toward him and lifted him. He cradled Mitts tightly with one arm while continuing to grasp the umbrella with his other hand.

Just then, the unexpected occurred. A forceful gust of wind suddenly swept along the sidewalk. It had the power of a hurricane! Xander and Mitts were lifted right off the ground. Xander held tightly to Mitts as both of them rose high into the air.

At first, Xander thought they would quickly fall back to the ground. Instead, he and Mitts stayed airborne, as the wind carried them all over their entire neighborhood! Xander's umbrella served as a kind of parachute that kept the pair aloft as they sailed up, up, and away.

Where in the world were they going?

Chapter 2

Dark and Light

The powerful windstorm continued.

Xander held tightly to Mitts with one arm as they flew high over the city. With his other hand, he kept a firm grasp on his umbrella.

"I can't believe this!" Xander cried.

Mitts barked with excitement. Xander looked at his dog and thought for a moment that his pug's eyes looked even

MORE wide open, as though Mitts couldn't believe what was happening either.

Xander didn't dare let go of his dog or his umbrella. If Mitts got away, who knew where he might be blown? If the umbrella came loose, both Xander and Mitts might crash to earth.

As the two flew even further, Xander noticed that the sky had grown dark. He could no longer see the city lights below. In fact, he couldn't see anything at all. No houses, no cars, no people!

It was pitch black.

It wasn't just the ground that was black. *Everything* around Xander was pure darkness. There were no clouds in the sky. The moon was gone, too! Xander couldn't see Mitts' face right in front of him!

Xander wished he could use the

flashlight on his belt to help him see. But with both hands occupied, he wasn't able to grab it.

"Hold on, Mitts!" Xander cried. "I know you're still with me. I can feel you!"

Xander and his dog sailed through the storm for what seemed like forever. Finally, the wind stopped.

Xander felt himself floating downward. He held onto Mitts extra tight.

It was still totally dark.

Xander wondered where he was. His feet felt wet. Soon, his whole body felt like it was floating in water. Mitts felt wet, too.

"Oh, Mitts!" Xander cried. "I hope we didn't land in the ocean! I don't know *what* we would do then!"

Mitts barked loudly. Xander remembered how his dog always barked whenever he got a bath at home.

"You probably think I'm bathing you now!" Xander said.

Mitts kept on barking. Xander held him tight to calm him.

Treading water, Xander had an idea. He was still holding his large, open umbrella. He placed it upside down in the water. Then he and Mitts carefully climbed over the edge and eased inside. The umbrella bobbed on the water like a small boat!

The umbrella continued to float along on the water. For a while, all was dark and quiet.

Then, Xander noticed a change. The darkness seemed to be disappearing slowly.

"Mitts, I think I see light!" Xander cried.

He waited anxiously to see if he was right.

"Yes, it *is* getting brighter!" Xander cried.

Mitts barked again with excitement. By now, Xander could see the outline of his dog's body. He leaned over and gave Mitts a big hug, and Mitts gave Xander some very wet, messy licks on the face. They were both relieved and began to breathe a little easier.

"Look, Mitts! Light, light!" he repeated.

Little by little, the light grew brighter and brighter. After a while, it had grown so bright that Xander needed to squint to adjust to it.

Slowly he opened his eyes and looked around. Xander couldn't believe it. He and Mitts *were* in water. And water was all they saw! Water, water everywhere!

Xander was puzzled. The setting was so strange, yet somehow it seemed familiar to him. How could that be? Xander knew that he had never been here before.

Soon, Xander noticed something even stranger. There was no sun in the sky. So, where was the light coming from?

Xander wanted to explore the area. But he couldn't. All he could do was stay put with Mitts in the umbrella and keep floating.

Xander didn't move for a long time. His body was soaked, yet he didn't feel chilled.

"I hope we don't get sick!" he said to Mitts. "Mom and Dad would really be mad at me for that!"

Xander began to think about home. By now his parents would realize he and Mitts were missing. A part of Xander wanted to return home so Mom and Dad wouldn't worry.

Yet another part of him wanted to stay to explore the area once they found land. *If* they ever found any land to explore!

"I wish I understood all this," Xander said to Mitts. "We were blown to a place filled with water and darkness. Then light appeared. Why does this all sound so familiar?"

Xander sighed, "Oh, Mitts, I guess we'll just have to call this Day One of our mysterious journey."

Suddenly, Xander had the answer. He snapped his fingers.

"Mitts!" he cried. "That's it -- Day One! *Now* I know why all this seems so familiar! I believe we've traveled back in time to the first day of the creation of the world!"

Chapter 3

Getting Separated

Xander quickly took out his compass. The dial indicated that they were travelling east. He knew that the creation of the world had taken place in the Middle Eastern part of the globe.

Xander couldn't believe it. He and Mitts had traveled in both space *and* time; eastward and all the way back to the first day of the world! It seemed so impossible. Yet now, everything made perfect sense.

At home, Xander had read Genesis, the first book of the Bible. It said that God created the world in six days.

"We've just experienced Day One," Xander said to Mitts. "That's when God created darkness and light."

That evening, Xander tried to remember what else he had read in the Bible. As he floated along the water in darkness and silence, he soon grew tired and nodded off with Mitts in his arms.

Xander slept for a long time, though he wasn't sure how long. When he awoke, he and Mitts were still inside their umbrella boat, bobbing on the water.

Xander was hungry. It occurred to him that he and Mitts hadn't eaten anything since they had left home.

Xander opened his canteen. It was filled with water.

He petted Mitts and said, "Well, pal, I guess we're going to have a liquid breakfast this morning."

Xander sipped some water from the canteen. It tasted cool and sweet. He drank more until he felt full.

Then he poured out some water for Mitts to lap up, too.

Xander checked his belt, maybe there was something useful in there. He found a couple of granola bars that he kept for times just like this. He opened one, and shared it with Mitts. Xander kept the other one for later.

Soon, Xander's thoughts returned to the Bible.

"I can't remember what happened on the second day of creation," Xander told Mitts. "But I have the feeling we'll be finding out very soon."

Xander was right. A short while later, the waters around him began to stir. Large waves rolled to the left and right. At first Xander feared that he and Mitts might be dragged under the water. He clutched his dog tightly.

"Hold on, Mitts," Xander said. "This may be a bumpy ride."

Xander balanced himself to keep from falling out of the umbrella.

The waters stirred more wildly. Mitts barked loudly at the crashing waves.

Suddenly, the waters began to swirl. Xander couldn't believe it! He watched as some of the water around him rose high into the air! It hovered above Xander's head. It looked like a flying ocean!

Xander gazed upward at the overhead sea. He worried that the waters above might suddenly come crashing down on him.

But that didn't happen.

Instead, the waters above stayed up in the sky. And there was still plenty of water below, where Xander was still floating with Mitts inside the umbrella.

When all the action stopped, Xander saw that a large, empty space had been created between the two sections of water.

"Look up, Mitts!" Xander cried. "It's the Heavens! Now I remember! That's what God created on Day Two -- the Heavens!"

Xander thought Mitts would bark -- but he didn't. Xander looked down. To his horror, Mitts was no longer in the umbrella!

Xander looked desperately at the waters around him.

"Mitts! Mitts!" he cried. "Where are you?" Tears started to fill his eyes.

Xander was very upset. He looked everywhere in the surrounding waters. Where was Mitts? When the waters swirled and separated, had Mitts fallen out of the umbrella and floated away?

Xander got out of the umbrella and swam in the waters around him. He searched everywhere for Mitts.

"Mitts! Mitts! Where are you?" he repeated.

After a long time, Xander grew tired and had to stop searching. He swam back to the umbrella and climbed inside. His eyes were red from the waters and from his own tears. He feared that his pet pug had drowned.

But Xander was wrong.

Suddenly, he heard barking. It

sounded like it was coming from above!

Xander looked up. He couldn't believe his eyes! There was Mitts, falling straight down from the Heavens! He looked like a sky-diving dog—only without a parachute! He was headed right for the waters below!

SPLASH! Mitts hit the water not too far from Xander. Xander quickly swam to him and grabbed the dog. Mitts barked happily.

Xander swam with Mitts back to the umbrella. They both climbed inside. Xander hugged and kissed his dog.

"Oh, Mitts, you're back!" Xander cried. "It's a miracle! Where in the world did you go?"

Mitts barked again and licked Xander's face.

Xander said, "You must have been carried upward when the waters separated to form the Heavens. And now you've come all the way back down!"

Xander hugged his dog for a long time.

"Oh, Mitts!" he cried. "I've heard of it raining cats and dogs. But today, it rained just one dog. And I'm so happy!"

Chapter 4

Flowers and Food

That evening, after a dinner of water and splitting the other granola bar, Xander slept soundly inside the umbrella. Mitts snuggled safely in his arms the entire night.

The next morning, Xander awoke early. His first thoughts were about Mom and Dad. They would surely be worried about him. Maybe they had even called the police. After this amount of time, Xander was now a missing person.

"Maybe we should try to get back home," Xander told Mitts.

Yet another part of Xander wanted to stay where he was. After all, this was the creation of the world! And no one in the world except Mitts and him had experienced it!

Besides, Xander thought, how would he get home, even if he wanted to? It's not like he could simply make himself fly back.

At that point, Xander stopped thinking about home. Instead, his thoughts returned to the Bible.

It was now Day Three. What had God created on that day? Xander couldn't recall. He only knew for sure that people weren't created until Day Six. So it would be a while before he met another human being.

Meanwhile, Xander was about to discover what was created on Day Three.

It began when the waters around him started to swirl again. Xander held Mitts tightly.

"You're not getting separated from me again!" Xander cried.

This time, however, the restless waters did not rise to the Heavens. Instead they parted, and Xander saw land appear between the waters.

"Land! Yes, that's it, Mitts!" Xander cried. "God created land on Day Three!"

Suddenly, Xander realized he and Mitts were no longer floating in the water. Instead, the umbrella was now sitting on dry land. NOW they had some exploring to do!

Xander and Mitts stepped out of the umbrella and onto the ground. Xander looked all around. In the distance, he could see the water.

"Look, Mitts, it's the sea!" Xander cried. "We're on land, not far from the sea!"

Mitts jumped out of Xander's arms. He raced ahead, barking loudly. Xander chased him.

"Come back, Mitts!" Xander called.

Xander chased Mitts for a long time. Suddenly, he couldn't see his dog anymore. In an instant, the land around him had changed. Instead of being bare ground, many plants, trees, and grass now appeared all around him!

Tall trees rose high into the air. Leafy green plants and colorful flowers sprouted from the ground.

Xander gazed in amazement to the left and to the right. Imagine...an instant jungle!

For a moment, Xander forgot completely about Mitts. He was too excited exploring all the vegetation. He found one bush with blueberries. They looked just like the berries that Mom used for baking pies.

Having only had water and a couple of granola bars the last two days, Xander felt hungry. He picked a large handful of blueberries and began to eat them. How juicy and sweet they tasted! This beat a breakfast of water and granola any day!

Immediately, Xander remembered Mitts. He must be hungry, too.

"Mitts, where are you?" he called.

Xander heard a bark. It sounded like it came from overhead. Xander looked up. There was Mitts--in a tree! The tree was leaning over at an angle, almost as if it could have been blown over during the

great winds of the storm that transported Xander and Mitts here in the darkness. Xander wasn't sure if somehow Mitts had climbed up the trunk and was now sitting on one of the tree's branches, or if the tree grew fast from right underneath Mitts!

"Mitts!" Xander cried. "How in the world did you get up there? You *never* climb trees at home!"

Xander called for Mitts to come down. But the dog just barked and stayed where he was.

"C'mon, Mitts, don't be stubborn," Xander said. "Come down from that tree right now. I'll give you some blueberries."

Xander held out a handful of berries for Mitts to see. The pug barked again, but didn't budge.

Xander realized he would have to

climb the tree himself to get Mitts down. He hugged the trunk and began to climb upward. Inch by inch, Xander made his way to the branch where Mitts sat.

"I can't believe you're making me do this, Mitts," Xander said. "And I thought we were friends."

After reaching the branch, Xander grabbed his dog and began to shinny back down the tree. At last, the two reached the bottom.

"Don't ever make me do that again, Mitts," Xander warned.

He brushed off the bark that had rubbed onto his clothing. Then he wiped his hands and fed Mitts some blueberries. The hungry dog ate them quickly.

"Too bad this isn't Mom's blueberry pie!" Xander laughed.

After eating, Xander held on to Mitts'

leash as the two explored more of the vegetation. Mitts sniffed the many flowers and plants around him.

When Mitts smelled a group of yellow daffodils, he barked again and again.

"I'll bet those flowers remind you of Mom's daffodils," Xander laughed. "They sure remind me."

Xander began to think again about going home. He knew his parents would never believe where he had traveled. How could he prove it to them?

Then Xander had an idea. He dug a handful of dirt from the earth and put it in his pocket.

"We can take this home to show Mom and Dad," Xander said to Mitts.

But Xander didn't express the rest of his thoughts aloud: "If we ever do get back home."

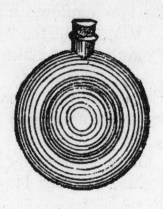

Chapter 5

A Full Sky

That night, Xander and Mitts slept on land for the first time since their travels had begun. A patch of soft grass served as their bed. It felt good.

The next morning, Xander noticed something very different about the world.

The sun was in the sky.

"Look, Mitts!" Xander cried, pointing

upward. "Now I remember what the Bible says happened on Day Four. That's when God created the sun."

Both Xander and Mitts felt the warmth of the giant yellow ball shining down on them. The dog barked excitedly. The warm sun was quickly becoming hot, like the middle of summer. It felt like the sun wanted to give its all on its very first day at work.

Xander began to tour the area with Mitts. He discovered even more trees, plants, and flowers than he had seen the day before.

"No climbing trees today," Xander warned Mitts with a smile.

The two walked a long time. Whenever Xander felt hungry, he stopped to pick fruits and berries off the trees and bushes. He shared each sweet treat with Mitts.

After walking a long time, the two reached a place where the land was met by water.

"We've come to the sea," Xander announced. "I can't believe we walked this far! Let's dip our feet in the water."

Xander took off his shoes and socks. The socks looked pretty dirty.

Xander had an idea. He put both socks into the water and rubbed them together.

"I officially declare Day Four to be Laundry Day!" he joked. "Mom would be proud of me for doing my own wash. Too bad God hasn't created detergent yet!"

When he was done washing his socks, Xander hung them on a nearby bush.

"The sun will dry them," he said.

Meanwhile, Xander and Mitts relaxed by the sea. Xander waded in the water up to his knees. He went no further, however. He wasn't sure if a fish might bite him.

"I don't think fish have been created yet," Xander said to Mitts. "But let's not take any chances."

Mitts placed one of his big front paws into the water. He barked and jumped up and down.

"I think you're enjoying yourself!" Xander said with a smile.

The rest of the morning and into the afternoon, Xander and Mitts explored more of the land. Everywhere they went, they discovered trees and plants with fresh fruits and berries. Xander especially loved the sweet, juicy peaches he had found.

After eating a lot, Xander began to feel sleepy.

"It's only the afternoon," he said. "But I feel like taking a nap."

He and Mitts found a nice bed of grass to rest upon. Soon they had both dozed off.

Some time later, Xander awoke. It was late afternoon. The sun was setting. Night was coming on.

Xander gazed at the sky. For the second time that day, he saw something in the Heavens that hadn't been there earlier.

He saw the moon.

Xander watched the moonlight as it shone on earth. He had learned in science class that the moon didn't give off its own light. Instead, it reflected the light from the sun.

Mitts began to bark at the moon.

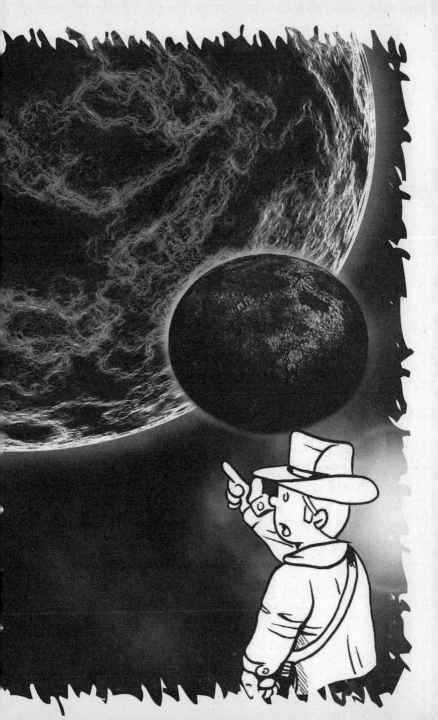

"Who do you think you are, Mitts," Xander joked, "a wolf howling at the moon?"

Just then, Xander also remembered that wolves and dogs were members of the same family. So even if Mitts wasn't an actual wolf, at least he was a cousin to one!

Soon, Xander noticed something else new in the sky. It was a star. How brightly it twinkled!

At first, Xander saw only one star. But as the sky grew darker, many more became visible.

Within minutes, thousands of sparkling, twinkling stars filled the sky.

"Look!" Xander cried. "That's more stars than I've ever seen in my life!"

Xander began to think about his very busy day. He'd seen the sun, the moon, and the stars. All of them had been created on Day Four.

Xander lay on his back, petting Mitts.

"Let's count the stars together," he said.

"One, two, three, four..."

Xander had almost reached two hundred when he fell asleep for the rest of the night. What Xander missed after nodding off were all the shooting stars filling the night sky, as if they were celebrating their own creation, like silent skyrockets launched from the hand of God.

Chapter 6

Swimmers and Fliers

When Xander awoke, it was the morning of Day Five. He and Mitts began what was by now their daily routine. They picked fruits and berries and ate breakfast.

Later, the two explored more of the land. They headed in a new direction. They walked through an area thick with trees and plants. Finally they came to a clearing.

Xander and Mitts heard chirping noises. Xander thought it sounded like birds.

He stepped out into a clearing and looked up. Sure enough, hundreds of birds were flying overhead! Small birds! Large birds! Birds of every color--orange, yellow, red, blue, and more!

Mitts barked and leaped up and down. He was trying to reach the flying creatures!

One of the birds--a white dove-- landed on the ground nearby. Mitts raced after it. The dove quickly rose and flew away.

"Mitts, you're scaring the birds!" Xander said, laughing. "Let them be."

Xander felt extra happy. At first he wasn't sure why. Then it struck him.

These were the first living creatures he had seen or heard -- besides Mitts -- in the past five days.

It felt good to see so many creatures moving about, Xander thought. He tried to identify as many birds as he could. He easily recognized the bluebirds, doves, and eagles.

He saw hummingbirds darting from one red flower to another, looking for drinks of nectar. He heard a familiar sound, and finally tracked down its source and spotted a red-headed woodpecker hammering on a tree with its beak.

Other birds were strange to Xander. He'd never seen them before. Xander had once read in a history book that some kinds of animals, like the Dodo bird, grew extinct after a long time. That meant they had died out completely.

As Xander gazed at the strange-looking birds, a thought occurred to him. Maybe some of these birds had died out long before he was born. If so, he was the only person from his generation ever to see them! Wow!

Xander continued to walk with Mitts. All along the way, more birds filled the sky.

Finally, Xander and Mitts came to a place where the land met the sea.

Xander heard splashing sounds in the water. It looked like raindrops were hitting the surface. Yet it couldn't be raining, Xander thought. He didn't see any dark clouds in the sky. He felt no rain on his body, either.

Xander bent down. He looked closely into the water. *Now* he knew what was causing the motion! He could see the outlines of fish swimming underwater!

"Look, Mitts!" Xander cried. "There

are so many fish in the water. Now I remember what God created on Day Five besides birds. He created fish!"

Then Xander remembered something else. It wasn't only fish that were in the water. According to the Bible, God had created other sea animals that weren't fish, such as whales and porpoises.

"Mitts, there are lots of different creatures in those waters," Xander explained.

Mitts edged closer to the water. He began to bark loudly at the fish. Xander could see them swimming away.

"Quiet, Mitts." Xander urged. "You're scaring the fish." And just then, almost as if to make the point, Xander saw pelicans just offshore crash-diving into the water trying to gulp up a few fish for lunch.

Xander held Mitts in his arms.

Gently, he stroked the dog, who remained quiet.

Soon, Xander saw the fish return.

"They look so peaceful," he whispered to Mitts.

That night, Xander thought about how Dad loved to go fishing. Xander had joined him a few times. However, he never got used to the idea of catching the fish with a hook. It was just too painful for Xander.

"I don't think we'll go fishing here, Mitts," Xander said softly before falling asleep. "Let's let the fish swim peacefully in their own home."

Chapter 7

Strange Noises

Xander awoke very early on the morning of Day Six. The rising sun brightened the land. Colorful birds filled the sky. Xander listened to them chirp and caw.

Xander felt extra excited this morning. He knew that Day Six was when God created Adam and Eve. Xander hoped that he would meet them soon. It would be nice to talk to someone who could answer in a way other than barking.

Xander found a nearby bush with raspberries. He picked a handful for breakfast. He shared the sweet treat with Mitts.

"Today's a big day," Xander announced. "Imagine meeting the very first people on earth!"

Mitts barked. Even he seemed excited about the idea.

After eating, Xander and Mitts began to walk among the trees.

"Keep your eyes open for Adam," Xander said. "He might appear any second."

After a while, Xander thought he heard something. It sounded like the rustling of leaves. Suddenly, he felt a little afraid. He and Mitts stood perfectly still.

"Adam?" Xander called in a shaky voice. "Is that you?"

EEEEEEEEEEERRRRRRRR!!!!!!

A loud shriek blasted nearby. The birds flew away in all directions.

Now Xander was really scared. He lifted Mitts and cradled him tightly.

"That doesn't sound like a person," Xander whispered.

EEEEEEEEEEERRRRRRRR!!!!!!

The shriek blasted again.

At first, Xander didn't see anything. Then he heard a different noise.

THUD! THUD! THUD! THUD!

It sounded like it was coming from behind the trees. No, it sounded like it

was coming *through* the trees, heading right towards him and Mitts, and it was getting louder!

Xander stood frozen.

Suddenly, a giant gray elephant stepped out into the clearing.

EEEEEEEEEEERRRRRRRR!!!!!!

Xander didn't move. He hoped the elephant wouldn't attack. He stood perfectly still.

Xander watched the elephant take a few more steps toward him. Just then, a herd of four more elephants paraded into the clearing.

All five elephants looked curiously at Xander and Mitts. After they came to a stop, as the dust was settling from their arrival, they all stood almost as still as Xander and Mitts. It was a stare-down.

Then the herd turned and walked away.

Xander breathed a sigh of relief.

"I guess they're not that interested in us," Xander told Mitts.

All was quiet for a moment. Then, without warning, a parade of other animals stepped out into the clearing. There were sheep, cows, donkeys, and horses, and more! A mixture of noises filled the air.

BAAAA! BAAAA!

MOOOOOOOOOOO!

HEE-HAW! HEE-HAW!

NEIGH!!

"It sounds like 'Old McDonald Had a Farm,' but without the music," Xander joked.

Just then, Xander realized something. He'd been so excited about meeting Adam and Eve that he'd forgotten what else God created on Day Six -- all the other animals after birds and fish. Everything from tall giraffes to tiny mosquitoes.

Xander saw colorful butterflies fluttering about him. Naturally, Mitts began to chase them, while barking.

"Don't even bother, Mitts," Xander laughed. "You'll never catch them!"

As Xander and Mitts roamed the area, they spotted even more animals. There were deer, goats, zebras, and bears. Xander was surprised by how well the animals got along with one another.

Suddenly, Mitts dashed into the woods. Xander started to chase after him. But just as quickly, Mitts returned to the clearing -- only now there were two Mittses!

Xander rubbed his eyes. He thought he was seeing double. Two dogs -- each looking exactly like Mitts -- stood before him.

Mitts must have found another pug in the clearing, Xander thought. An identical pug!

Now Xander had a problem. Which Mitts was his?

Xander cried, "Here, Mitts!"

Both dogs raced toward him. They licked his face. Xander still didn't know which one was his dog.

Then he thought, I'll know the sound of his bark.

"Okay, Mitts," Xander said to both pugs. "Woof, woof! Bark for me!"

Both pugs barked. They sounded

identical.

Xander looked puzzled. He stood quietly, trying to tell the animals apart.

Just then, Xander heard a voice from the woods. It called, "Dog!"

One of the two pugs turned and ran toward the woods. The other pug stayed by Xander's side.

A male figure stepped out into the clearing. His dog stood next to him. The man was naked, but seemed at ease and unembarrassed. Xander remembered from Genesis how Adam and Eve were naked after God created them.

Xander was stunned. Slowly, the man approached him. Xander WAS embarrassed, though, and his heart was pounding in his ears and chest. Quickly though, Adam's own comfort put Xander at ease.

"Adam?" he asked shyly.

"Yes," the stranger replied, staring at Xander. "Who are you?"

Xander couldn't believe it. He was actually speaking with Adam, the very first person on earth, created just hours earlier!

"My name is Xander Nash," Xander explained.

"Xander?" Adam repeated. "I've been naming God's creatures all morning, but I don't remember naming one Xander."

Xander smiled. "It's short for Alexander," he said.

"I don't remember Alexander, either," Adam said. "Did God just create you?"

"No," Xander explained. "I wasn't created just now. I'm nine years old."

Adam looked puzzled.

"You're nine years old?" he asked. "How is that possible? God told me this morning that the world is only six days old."

"Yes, that's true," Xander tried to explain. "But I come from the future."

Xander saw that Adam didn't understand what he was saying. Xander wasn't sure he even understood it himself!

"Six days ago, I traveled back in time," Xander continued. "I'm not sure how I did it, but I arrived here."

Adam looked at Mitts. "And who is that?" he asked.

"That's my dog, Mitts," Xander said. "He traveled here with me."

Adam petted his own dog. "My dog

looks the same as yours," Adam said. "But I call mine Dog, not Mitts. Perhaps these two animals belong to the same family."

Xander nodded and said, "They do." Then he quickly added, "You and I belong to the same family, too. We are both human beings."

"So you are my relative, Alexander?" Adam asked. "Are you my son?"

"No," Xander laughed. "You don't have any sons -- at least not yet. I'm more like your great-great-great-great-great-grandson, only with many more greats. Too many to list."

Adam put his arm around Xander. "Welcome to the family, Alexander," he said. "Come with me. Let me introduce you to another member of our family."

Chapter 8

A Tough Choice

Xander and Mitts followed Adam through the woods. After a while, they came to a cave.

Adam called, "Eve!"

Suddenly, a woman stepped out of the cave. She looked surprised to see Xander and Mitts. Xander, looking to Eve's face, drew in a breath and looked away out of

respect as he expected that she too would be naked. Eve, though, like Adam, seemed unashamed and not at all embarrassed.

Then Xander noticed something. However Eve moved, she was always covered properly to Xander's line of sight. Either she was behind a boulder, a tree branch, or an animal walked between them. Knowing Xander would be embarrassed, God was clearly looking out for him, making it so that he could meet and talk to Eve without having to avert his eyes. Realizing that God was taking care of this made Xander much more comfortable.

"Are these God's newest creations?" Eve asked Adam.

"No," Adam explained. "This is Alexander, and that is his dog, Mitts. They come to us from the future."

"What does future mean?" Eve asked

with a puzzled look.

Xander tried to explain, just as he had done with Adam. Like Adam, she didn't seem to understand completely.

"Alexander, would you like to eat something?" Eve asked.

"No, thank you," Xander said quickly. He remembered that the Bible described how Adam and Eve ate the Forbidden Fruit and were punished for it. But he knew all of that wouldn't happen until later.

"Will you stay with us here?" Adam asked. "Or will you go back to the future?"

Xander began to think about his family. He missed Mom and Dad a lot. He even missed his brother Kevin. Yet here he was experiencing an amazing journey that no one else had ever taken.

"I'm...not sure," Xander muttered. "I think I'd like to be with my family again, but I don't know how to make it happen."

Eve looked at Xander. "How did you get here?" she asked.

Xander described the rain and windstorm that had blown Mitts and him from their home.

Adam smiled. "I know how you can go back," he said.

Xander was shocked. "How?" he asked.

"God created me from the dust of the earth," Adam explained. "He breathed into my nostrils, and I became alive. It was the breath of life."

Xander looked puzzled. "What does that have to do with me?" he asked.

Adam smiled again. "I arrived in this world through God's breath," he said.

"You did, too, Alexander, only you called it a windstorm. Remember, Alexander, the wind is just another form of God's breathing."

Xander scratched his head. He had never thought of the wind in that way.

Adam continued, "If God's breath brought you here, then it can also take you back home as well."

"But how?" Xander asked.

"You just need to ask God to do it," Adam replied. "If you ask sincerely, I believe he will answer your prayer."

Xander was quiet for a long time. He thought about Adam's advice. Pray to God to return to his family. Was that all he really had to do?

Xander looked at Mitts.

"Do you want to return home, Mitts?"

he asked.

Mitts barked.

"I'll take that as a yes," Xander said.

Then Xander turned to Adam and Eve.

"I'm going to take your advice," he said. "If my prayers are answered, then I'd better say goodbye to you now."

"Until next time," Adam said.

"What do you mean?" Xander asked.

Adam explained, "If you traveled here once, it might happen again."

"In the future," Eve added, smiling.

Xander realized they were right.

"Then I'll say goodbye to you . . . for now," he replied.

Adam and Eve waved to Xander and Mitts. "Take care, Alexander," they said together.

Even Adam's dog and Mitts said goodbye. They rubbed their faces together.

"Okay, Mitts," Xander said. "Let's go."

Xander and his dog walked back to the place where they had slept the night before. Xander checked his explorer's belt to make sure it held his flashlight, compass, map, and writing pad.

He tugged his faithful fedora firmly on his head, so that it would not fall off.

Then he grabbed his large umbrella and opened it.

"This may come in handy again," he told Mitts.

When Xander was ready, he took a

deep breath and faced the Heavens.

Xander said, "Dear God, you allowed Mitts and me to take such an incredible journey. Thank you. We are so grateful for that."

Xander paused and then continued. "But now it's time for us to return home. Home to my family. Please send us back home now, God."

Xander held tightly to Mitts. At first, all was quiet. The land remained calm.

Then, suddenly there was a powerful burst of wind -- like a hurricane. It was so strong that Xander's fedora almost blew away.

Xander held Mitts tightly as the fierce wind lifted both of them into the air. He grasped the umbrella as tightly as he could.

"That's God's breath!" Xander cried to

Mitts. "God is breathing hard to send us back home!"

Mitts barked with excitement.

In an instant, the two were up in the clouds, high over the land.

Chapter 9

The Final Surprise

Xander and Mitts flew quickly as the powerful wind blew them westward. Xander looked down on the land as they sailed overhead. What an experience he'd had below! He wondered if he'd made the right choice by returning home after only six days.

Then Xander thought about his parents. He knew they would be relieved to see him once again.

Xander lost track of time as he and Mitts traveled in the sky. Eventually, he noticed that it was completely dark.

Xander petted Mitts. "Don't worry, I'm still here, Mitts, even though we can't see each other," he said.

After a very long time, Xander gasped. The darkness was gone. He could see land below! Only it wasn't the land of Adam and Eve. It was Xander's own neighborhood!

"Hold on, Mitts!" Xander cried. "I think we're coming in for a landing!"

The winds slowed down, and Xander and Mitts slowly floated to earth. They landed gently on the sidewalk, right in the exact same spot where they had been lifted up and carried away six days earlier.

Xander looked at his watch. It was the

same time of day as when he had left. Only now, there was no rain or windstorm.

"We're home, Mitts, home!" Xander cried.

Mitts barked and licked Xander's face.

The two raced quickly for several blocks until they reached their house. Xander thought he might see police cars outside. But everything looked normal.

Xander opened the front door and walked inside.

"Hello!" he called. "Is anybody home?"

Mom stepped out of the kitchen.

"Alexander, you're back so soon?" she asked.

Just then, his father walked into the

room.

"Hello, son," he said. "How was your walk with Mitts?"

Xander was confused. He ran to Mom and Dad and hugged them both.

"I'm so glad to see you!" he cried. "I was afraid you'd be so worried about me."

Dad smiled. "Why would we be worried?" he asked. "You just went for a walk with Mitts."

"But that was six days ago!" Xander exclaimed. "Didn't you miss me?"

Mom looked puzzled. "Six days ago?" she said. "What are you talking about, Alexander? You just left the house about a half an hour ago."

Mom looked closely at Xander. "Are you feeling all right, dear?" she asked.

Xander shook his head.

"No!" he insisted. "I've been gone for six days. Mitts and I took an incredible journey. The wind blew us all the way back to the creation of the world. I met Adam and Eve!"

Mom smiled as she felt his forehead. "Alexander, I think you should lie down," she suggested.

Xander sat on the sofa. He didn't understand why Mom and Dad hadn't missed him all week.

Then, suddenly, it struck Xander.

"*Now* I understand!" Xander blurted. "Mom, Dad, you couldn't know I was gone because I time-traveled. I returned at the exact same time as when I left. So it never seemed to you like I was gone at all!"

Dad nodded. "Of course, son," he said,

"whatever you say."

"But, but . . . my socks are clean." Xander blurted. He wasn't sure how else he could prove what he was saying.

Just then, Kevin walked into the house.

"Well, it's the great explorer," Kevin joked. "Too bad you didn't see the movie with me, Xander. It was great. A giant marshmallow ate the whole city of Cleveland!"

Xander smiled. "Where did the marshmallow come from?" he asked.

"I dunno," Kevin admitted. "I missed the beginning of the movie. But it doesn't matter. All the exciting stuff happened at the end of the story."

Xander laughed. "Well, Mitts and I saw the beginning. The *very* beginning!"

Kevin looked confused. "You mean *you* were at the movie, too? And they let Mitts into the theater??"

Xander laughed again. "No," he explained. "Mitts and I traveled back to the beginning of the world. We experienced the first six days of creation. *That's* the beginning I mean!"

Kevin had a funny look. "Yeah, right," he said. "Xander, you've sure got a wild imagination."

Suddenly Xander remembered the dirt in his pocket. He pulled out a handful to show Kevin and his parents.

"Here!" Xander cried. "This is real dirt taken from the first earth ever created!"

"Alexander!" Mom cried. "Don't get the carpet dirty!"

"Oh, come on," Kevin said, pushing Xander's hand away. "You could've scooped up that dirt from our backyard. Who do you think you're fooling?"

Xander looked at Mitts. "They don't believe us, Mitts. But we *did* go back to the beginning, didn't we, pal?" he said.

Mitts barked and jumped up and down.

Xander didn't care that no one believed his story. He knew it was all true.

He hoped Adam and Eve were right. Maybe Xander and Mitts *would* be able to return for another visit soon.

But most of all, Xander knew that Kevin was definitely wrong. The most exciting stuff *does* happen in the beginning!

Dr. Hunter Talen, is a fictional character that was born in either 1947 or 1625. He was raised by his globetrotting archaeologist father, G. Therer Talen, and his mother Katherine "Kat" Klause-Talen, who had been a singer in silent films. He was exposed to many of the great archaeological sites across 5 continents before the age of ten. He attended *Der Spelunken Academy* in Gestalt and studied under the world renowned explorer Dr. Heverford "Ever" Last, graduating with his PhD at 17. By 20 he had already done extensive work translating the runes of the Upper Tribes of Invisiline and published his findings on the secret rituals of the Gurl Skowtz in three best selling volumes, all to international acclaim.

Talen inspired countless field archaeologists with his works, and has been awarded a *Pica Star* by the Adventuring Fellowship out of Genova. He has earned three "Bom Diggity" awards and is a member of the exclusive Secret Adventurers Club and of the surprisingly less exclusive Top Secret Adventurers Club. He currently calls the outer rim of the Mauna Lisa volcano home and base of operations in between expeditions.

Neil Kleid, the Xeric-Award winning cartoonist, authored *Ninety Candles*, *Brownsville*, and *The Big Kahn*. Neil has written for Marvel, DC, Dark Horse and Image Comics, Shadowline, NBM Publishing, Archaia Studios, Slave Labor Graphics, Random House and Puffin Graphics. He lives in New Jersey with his wife and kids, working on three graphic novels, several comic books, a novel and no sleep. Pray for him at www.rantcomics.com

Creation By Design's mission is to create educational and entertaining Biblical products that help children connect with God's word in an exciting, fun way. Using the latest in computer digital graphics, Creation By Design offers our children the images they are interested in and want to see, and offers parents a new way for our next generation to bond with Scripture. Come see what is new at www.creationbydesign.com

XANDER NASH:

HAS AN ADVENTURE JUST FOR YOU!

ISBN: 978-0-9828077-5-0

ISBN: 978-0-9828077-6-7